A Clever Arrangement Of Words

L10 !

Made with ❤ on the BookLeaf Publishing Platform

www.bookleafpub.in

www.bookleafpub.com

Dedication

To anyone and everybuddy who reads this book. Anybuddy with a spark in their heart. And most importantly to all of those four legged friends.

Preface

Word Vomit...

Acknowledgements

An exhausting waltz
always lost in thought.
Please bury me in Spanish moss.

1. Words

Okay okay,
here I go...

Unsure really to begin,
so I will just start throwing
words around hoping for
some sort of sentence structure...

Or at least
some sort of profound thought
inside of this brain I got...

2. Esspressing Grief

Woke up to the burn of a brewed brain.
A caffeinated clockwork to drive me insane.
I pour my heart into these cups,
but they are always overflowing.
The taste it lingers
and I just keep going.

Sipping coffee all alone in my room,
stuck inside of this over caffeinated gloom.
Coffee cup confessions,
sometimes the
ending comes too soon.

Roasted memories collide,
stirring the pot,
brewing feelings I can not hide.
Through the steam,
I can see your face.

Haunted by the smiles
that we can not replace.
Too bitter to consume,
yet I sip the memories.
A bittersweet taste.

3. An Honest Exhaustion

It's been 52 weeks

and

it seems like the tv

is always blaring,

but

I can't hear a sound -

except the fading memory of your laughter.

Fragmented fabrications holding on tightly

as the threads slowly unravel.

A warm embrace that is never at peace.

Time is a thief, stealing your presence,

and

leaving me with all these pieces.

Sinking deeper into my sheets.

This bed feels like a graveyard

and

I don't dream anymore.

I don't have the time too.

These empty pages remind me

of this paper thin reality.

I am tracing out the silence.

The colors fade just like the words

I forgot to speak.
Days swallowed whole by the weight
of untimely goodbyes.
I'll scribble down all these verses
but
I'll choke on the words.

It all begins to blur,
illuminating this phantom pain
where your smile should be.
Starting to feel desperate like a prayer,
I'm just left gasping for air.
A pain in my chest,
a mess suffocating in sheets,
caught in a loop.
I'm still here
and
I wish you would haunt me.

4. Dear Abby

Have you ever tried to just be yourself?
Some days that feels like a prison cell.
It's so easy to be a poet crafting verses,
metaphors borrowed,
but oh so hard to be a person,
and walk around this skin that I'm in.

Learning to find the truth in my flaws,
the strength when I'm weak.
Finding new adjectives to help me adjust
and you know there's never enough verbs -
but I'll tell you what -
The best advice I ever heard

" One step at a time, it's brave to be alive."

5. Have You Ever Been Bitten By A Wolf?

I've been sleeping too much;
or is it never enough?
By the time the wolf howls,
the clock strikes noon
and I've already had enough.
Sick to my stomach,
chewing all of these secondhand thoughts.
Keep on running from the things
that used to mean something.

Keep on shedding my skin,
searching for the prize.
The only difference between a ghost hunt
and a ghost chase is your frame of mind -
Sun up, sun down, ain't no sunshine
at the end of the day,
only the moon to take my breath away.
Howling out

"I've been over my head more than one time.
Can some one please tell me
why the weight of being human
feels so hauntingly bright? "

6. You Are What You Eat

I am every thought
you have ever had.
I am everything you hold dear.
I am everything you wish you could be.
I am everything wrong with society.
I am nothing at all.
I am the graffiti cocks in a bathroom stall.
I am the voice that keeps you up at night.
I am all the words that you couldn't speak.
I am all the promises you couldn't keep.
I am boredom on the week days while
watching the paint dry.
I am that mundane feeling you get day after day.
I am the arms on a clock always ticking by.
I am the kiss on your forehead
that starts and ends each and every day.
I am everything that you say.
I am everything that you think.
Don't you know you'll always be haunted.
I am all that pulls you down.
I am the reason you'll never forget
that everything is fucked.

7. An Honest Proposition

With a heart full of chaos
and no one to blame but myself -
I'll light up another,
feel the burn begin to creep down.
Lost in the silent sound,
I'd amputate it all until
I'm nothing left but stumped.
Just like my cough I am only getting worse -
there's a beauty in the choke -
but I will continue to hold onto hope
just like I hold on to all these cigarette butts.

8. Have You Ever Fallen?

So leave the TV on,
I'll be sure to be quick..

Watching the static,
my thoughts feeling too thick -
in this city of dreams,
I'm just slipping through the cracks.
Losing track of time and space
holding hands in your bed,
just two skeletons
with crooked spines intertwined.

Counting stars on the darkest night.
Two souls entwined
like cigarette smoke in the wind.
Held captive in your lungs
all the air we share.
Tangled in this space,
clinging bone to bone.

Shooting stars fall hard.
Come on my little jet pack,
let's fly far above all the noise.

9. Carried Away in Silence

Crossbow teeth
and
hands made of
freeze dried apathy.
A spit shine clean
followed by
the reform -
its been such
a long time
since that cold day -
I'm ready for
another drink.
Lack of sympathy
and
all these hallowed
out memories.
Black out drunk again
up by Lake Michigan
and
you know that
I can't swim -

Please bury me
in smashed beer cans

and
holy snail trails.
Listen now.
Guitar solos
and screaming ferals.
A beat in my head
or
a palp in my heart?
Either way
I'm on the
dance floor tonight.
All these
unsolved mysteries
and
feelings of sanctuary-
Please tell me
Mister Stack
is this a black hole
in my mind
or
just my wrist?

I lost my lungs
coughing up
all my dreams -
I am a one man
Apollo mission -

An Astro-nut-
burning up in the stars.
Scratch out my eyes
and
lead me to
watering holes..

Holding my
hands out for
strangers with candy -
god damn it
I'm just trying
to settle my
sweet tooth,
meth mouth,
chatter box,
shit smile grin
always chomping.
Cut it up
and
hum out loud
a tune
a nothing
a something
into everything -

Wasting away

just like last year.
What the hell is content?
What happens to comfort?
Will we ever grow up
or
just learn to tie knots?
I'm getting too old
for this shit
and
you know
I'd be lying
if I said trust me
but I've got
nothing left to lose
in this hand of cards
I've been dealt -
suicide kings
and
strung out queens
I'm not just a fool..
pissing on sticks
and
sipping on vinegar.
Well wishing
and
wondering if
I should get high

behind the couch
in the backyard -

I can't tell if
I'm jaded
or
only scarred
from a tragic game
of lawn darts -
Here's an idea
better
make it quick -
Right through the head
like lighting -
only much hotter
and
so full of vain.

I said everything
would work out -
but digging is
never deep enough..
A violent police chase
filled up
with speed
and
nothing but grace -

If we make this one
out alive
I'll buy you
a whole god damn island
and
we can watch
our sorrows swim
inward
to the shoreline
where the seagulls
greet them with screams
and
threats to peck out the rest.

10. Triumphs of the Human Body

I am over 60% water and just floating.

Roughly 37.2 trillions cells make up
this body and not one of them feel right.

206 bones stuffed tightly into my skin.
The largest organ of them all and the
most uncomfortable.

Over 7 trillion nerves and every which one of them on
their last.

Over 100 beats a minute and this heart
is not slowing down.

Unsure of how many muscles,
I just need enough
to leave this room.

11. The Way You Cried to Toy Story Three

Tangled in my head,
just a whisper lost
in the decay.
Fever dream filled swamp,
self mutilation
razor blade simulation -
cutting through looking for relief.

What's it's called when
everything just feels incomplete?
My time is just on lease
and
I'm running out of song lyrics
to believe.

Living in a natural devotion
to a never ending corrosion
of emotions...
and I'm froze in fear.

I tried to understand the pretty
piece of shit that is me,
but -

everything just gets swollen
in this head filled with locust.

Caught in the loop
of the coldest moment.
Shitty metaphors to decipher
the unnoticed.
What's another word for
a chronic hyper focused symbiotic neurotic
melodramatic symbolic piece of shit?

I'm oh so sorry for the mess,
I just have so much
to get off my chest.
Empty bottles rattle
and
the wind howls along -

With the shades drawn shut
the sun doesn't come around anymore.
Deep breathing focusing
on my consumption of oxygen.
I really should tell my friends
I love them more.

12. How I Stopped Being Addicted to Legalized Gambling and Learned to Love Myself

I loved you plenty
like I tried to love myself.
I felt the sun shine
and
now I'm drowning
in the moons tide.

Pulled beneath the waves,
where the shadows try to hide.
Time slips by
and
I'm still
caught in my own head -
living in the echoes,
of the things I hope you know
and the things I wish said.

Now I'm just a
vessel of the pencil.
A creature with
detrimental sentimental ties ,
screaming in the silence
trying to feel alive -
in this world
that feels so empty.

Wrapped in disdain.
I reach out for
something tangible
but it slips
through my hands
like the curve
of your clavicle..

The weight of
all these what ifs
and
if wishes were fifths,
then we'd both be sure,
to drown our conversations
in oceans of regret.

A lonely confession,
pour me another

and
we can place bets.

Pour it heavy
and
let it spill into
this fragile existence.
With the bottle
as my witness,
I'd trade in
all these moments
of regret
for a moment
of your truth.

Ink stained fingers,
a tequila muse,
and every picture
I ever drew.
If only a bottle could
wash it all true -
I'd trade it all
for another moment with you.

So pour me another -
and
we can drown

in what we've missed
and
seal it
with a kiss.
Lets let's drink
to the moments
where we both fell apart.
Losing ourselves
in this bittersweet art.
Love is a lot
like Russian roulette
Pour me another,
it's a safe bet.

13. An Honest Discussion

The heart can be a weapon,
but it can crack under hope.
So I'll deconstruct this life I've made,
each broken piece, a masquerade.
These memories dance like cigarette ash.
Smoke lingers, but nothing ever last.
And I can feel the weight of all the words never said.
Cigarette burns and a melting clock -
time sure flies when you're shit
- Fuck -
Maybe I should just go out for a walk.
Contemplate what I've become,
the friends I entrust.
Papier-mâché intrusive remarks,
wrist glued shut
and a heart made of art.

14. You Are Art

In the vast cosmos
where minds can collide -
our paths intertwined
with emotions implied.

What is the human connection
if not a fusion of souls,
navigating through
time and space.
As the story unfolds
dancing on the edges
of cosmic seas -
where heartbeats resonate
like symphonies wrapped
in a tapestry of feelings
entangled in the air -
Defying boundaries
beyond one's compare.

From the highest of highs
or
the lowest of lows -
we oscillate
and

we sway,
passing through
laughter and tears
from joy to sadness.
A kaleidoscope of hues,
intersecting vessels
woven throughout time.

Emotions in motion,
celestial signs -
we are but just dots
forever changing on
this boundless plane.
Finding connections
in vulnerability.
Come what may,
it is in our own
complexities
where we find solace
and peace.
Each and every interaction
another masterpiece.

15. A Tad Bit About Me

In this murky pond,
the great unknown -
I find myself
yearning to be a
tadpole.

With no legs
to call my own.
Segments of my life
disintegrate into shame-
dragged down in vain.
I am just
a fragile creature
lost in a world
that is so vast.
Bound by my inner own flaws,
I feel myself fading fast.

Each step I take
seems to dig me
deeper down -
these memories claw
at my mind -
leaving these scars behind.

But if I could rewind,
just go back to
simpler days,
maybe then
I could find solace
in the
amphibious haze.

I want to be
a tadpole -
with no legs to lead the way.
Drifting in these troubled waters
where I truly belong.
I want to be a tadpole.

16. Unwritten

Letters left unread,
memories fading black.
Standing pigeon toed, freaking out,
lost out in the old green field.

Letter to carry home,
but the ink has lost its yield.
These empty words,
they just fall flat.
Lost feeling in my bones,
but my mind...
I can't get **you** out of that.

17. Austin 3:16

Tried to smile today,
it was a total flop.
It's been one hell of a year
and
it's only March.
Three months in,
but
I'm feeling six feet deep.

I could use a drink.

Get lost in a tall boy can.
A toast to my troubles
and
to the dreams I never wrote.
To all my unhealthy coping,
and the tears I couldn't cry.
To the chaos,
to the mess I hold dear.
This year maybe a glass half-empty,
but
I'm sippin' on a cold beer,
pouring one out for the one's
we'll never forget.

It's been one hell of a year
but
I'm not done yet.

18. What The Fuck Is Going On?

I've got laundry that needs done
there's clothes left to fold
and bills to pay.
Families are dying,
and war is no place
for children to play.
I've got friends going
to their children's games
and friends hooked up
to breathing machines.
I should brush my teeth,
while there's been
more bombings,
than I've got teeth left.
The politicians are
always lying,
I've got chores to do
and people are dying.
Have you ever cried
in front of birds,
when the world
continues to turn?
The rich are get richer

while we fight over
culture wars
distractions from the truth,
speaking from thumbs
and hiding behind booze.
I'm told this is just
the way things are,
too make my bed
but I'm pretty sure
it's no conspiracy
that there is too much hate
in this place
it's not just in my head.

19. Muse

Painted radiance.
Every stroke of your soul,
captivating me.

In this artful madness,
you're the masterpiece I find.

Caught in the canvas
of you embrace,
bound by the brushes,
of fates design.

Timeless connection,
as the stars align.
Sealed with endless scars,
just like the sun and the moon
I'd swallow the void for you.

A tortured artist,
consumed by your spark.
A modern renaissance dream,
with beauty that rivals
the heavens up high,
etched deep in my mind's foundation.

We're are but melting colors,
a beautiful mess,
a symphony of chaos,
our hearts coalesce.

20. How Are You?

This weight I carry,
bittersweet.
I'm lost in echoes, dragging my feet.
Every smile feels like a disguise,
And
every negative thought just amplifies,
The voice that whispers in my head -

"Why even bother? Just join the dead."

I know it's all wrong,
but
I feel like dying again.

A
shallow shell just waiting for my end.
I'll wear my scars like a badge of pride
but if we are being honest -
deep down I just want to hide.
A
lonely ghost in a crowded room
full of lost souls,
in the midst of the laughter,
I'm lost in despair,

searching for comfort
in the stripes that I wear.

I know it's all wrong,
but the urge is so strong,
to fade into silence.
This collateral damage
my heart a fragile thread
unraveling at the thought of death.
Little constant reminders -
I'm lost in decay.

My relentless self pity parade -
living life an existential masquerade.
A
hollow existence,
where it feels like I don't belong.
With this weight that I carry,
I feel myself sinking...

I know it's all wrong
but -

it's getting hard to pretend
that I haven't been thinking
about dying again.

21. You Are Lisa Simpson

Life can get really heavy sometimes,
and
honestly I feel like giving up a lot -
but
in the darkest hours,
I hear a whisper clear,

"Hold on to the moments,
sweet time is sincere."

and

I'm thankful for all the times I didn't.
You see life's a collection of moments,
sweet and bittersweet,
with a lesson in every heart beat.

Life can be heavy
it's a burden,
it's true -
but
I'll carry the weight
if it means I get to see you.